Table of CONTENTS

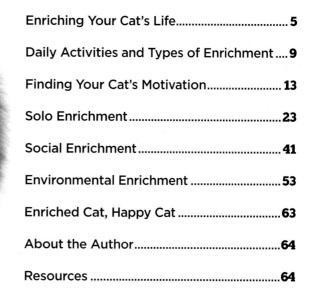

WHEN CAPTIVE POLAR BEAR Gus began exhibiting obsessive-compulsive behaviors, zookeepers were told he needed something to do. Like Gus, a bored, anxious, or stressed domestic cat requires enriching activities to keep him healthy and happy.

Enriching Your CAT'S LIFE

While on a visit to the zoo, a cat lover will certainly include a trip to admire the lions, tigers, and cougars in their mini jungles. It's amazing to see these giant cats groom themselves, amuse themselves with tree branches, and wrestle with one another. Every behavior seems to mirror that of house cats, so who would think that feline fanatics would learn even more about their pets by watching a polar bear?

In the mid-1990s, zookeepers at the Central Park Zoo in New York City noticed that their 700-pound male polar bear, Gus, seemed to be experiencing some stress. Gus swam back and forth in his small pool day after day, for hours on end. Clearly, something was dreadfully wrong with the bear, so the zoo hired an animal behaviorist to study him. What was the diagnosis? Years of captivity had caused Gus to become neurotic, and his obsessive-compulsive behaviors most likely were meant to keep him from going out of his mind from boredom. This natural predator wanted something to do.

The behaviorist suggested that the Central Park Zoo implement a protocol of enrichment activities and create an environment that would stimulate the natural tendencies of the polar bear and break his neurotic patterns. So the zookeepers installed a whirlpool for Gus, began offering his food in packages for him to open, hid food around his habitat for him to hunt down, froze fish in giant blocks of ice for him to break open, and gave him interactive toys to play with. Gus seemed to be thrilled with all of these additions to his habitat. He stopped his pointless swimming as he learned to play and forage as he would in the wild. That's what enrichment is all about: keeping your pet active and engaged in his environment.

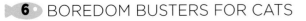

Enrichment for cats means anything—a toy, a game, an adventure—that stimulates natural behavior, keeping them active and engaged. Many behavioral problems can be solved by adding these types of activities to your cat's life and environment. As with Gus, lack of enrichment can cause stress and anxiety, which a cat may express with excessive grooming or inappropriate elimination.

Enrichment can eradicate, or lessen, these problems and other ones, including antisocial behavior and obesity. This book explores a number of simple ways you can provide your cat with stimulating enrichment to keep him happy, healthy, and out of trouble.

(*Warning*: always watch your cat when he plays with stringy toys, such as the one above, which he could chew, choke, and/or eat and end up with an intestinal obstruction.)

Daily Activities and

TYPES OF ENRICHMENT

Wanting to know what to expect is natural for a cat, an animal needing routine for comfort and security. Studies of feral, or community, cats (who differ from stray cats in that they were never socialized as kittens and were never pets) reveal that they are either solitary animals who stay within a defined territory or members of colonies that reside close to a food source, choosing to deal with each other for survival's sake. Day after day, these animals know what to expect and how to fend for themselves. The average feral cat is one tough cookie! Thriving packs of wild dogs are far rarer than healthy feral cat colonies.

Even though feral cats are the same species of cat that lives in your home, there's one important difference: the house cat is not in charge of his own life. Without prey to hunt, other cats to compete with, and the daily struggle for basic survival, the house cat must rely on his humans to give him order and activity. Cats, like most animals, evolved with a purpose; they have natural instincts that tell them what to do.

If you don't enrich your cat's environment, then these instincts may stray toward activities such as clawing your furniture and overgrooming. You wanted your home to have that lived-in clawed look, right? Very fashionable.

There are three types of enrichment activities for cats—solo, social, and environmental; your cat will do best when you engage him in activities of all types. Although your cat likes routine, within that routine he needs variety to keep him interested in what you have to offer.

Solo: Solo activities encourage your cat to engage in an activity alone. Seeking and catching prey motivates most cats, so they like moving or noisy objects they can run after. Food also motivates many cats, so they may enjoy eating from food-dispensing toys rather than their food bowls. Most cats have a variety of motivations that you can tap into to create solo enrichment activities.

Social: Social enrichment involves interactions between your cat and you, other people, and possibly dogs and other cats (depending on your cat's level of sociability). Opportunities for social enrichment include engaging in games that simulate hunting prey, cuddling, spending safe time outside, and training.

Environmental: Enriching your cat's environment to give him activity options will provide much-needed exercise for the couch-kitty and give your cat mental stimulation, which decreases feline depression and boredom. Environmental enrichment may include giving him a dedicated space in which to play, entertaining things to watch (such as the birds outside), and high perches from which to survey his world.

Finding Your Cat's
MOTIVATION

What's your cat's personality? Is your cat outgoing, shy, bossy, a professional sunbather, a territorial terror, a love sponge—or are you in a household with multiple cats, whose personalities include several of the above? You can choose your cat's ideal enrichment activities by categorizing him to discover what kinds of toys and games he is most likely to appreciate. On the following pages, you'll find a list of common cat personality traits and some of the toys and activities these kitties will revel in and get the most enrichment out of.

A lionhearted cat sees something "pounceable" in his weedy jungle. For safety, only let a cat play alone outdoors in a secure enclosure.

The lionhearted cat doesn't just think he is a lion— he knows that he is. He is king of the (household) jungle, lord of all he surveys.

The bossy cat: This particular feline rules over other pets and humans with an iron paw. He will benefit from food-dispensing toys and from high perches, where he can oversee everything going on in the house.

The hunter: This kitty will bless you for adding a window bird feeder to his repertoire of daily things to watch and dream about. Laser toys, feathers, and toys that swing, bounce, and move radically will enchant the hunter. Do make sure he "wins" his game sometimes so he doesn't get frustrated. Camouflage optional.

The "let's share" cat: Actually, this cat is less "let's share" and more "what's yours is mine, what's mine is mine, and what's over there is mine, too." You lay your head down on your pillow at night only to find him already ensconced there. Want to sit in your favorite chair? Not so fast; there's a cat lounging in it. No matter—he's cute enough to get away with this behavior! This cat loves things with your scent on them and to be near you, so allow for plenty of cuddling time.

The lionhearted cat: The lionhearted cat doesn't just think he's a lion—he knows that he is. He is king of the (household) jungle, lord of all he surveys. Provide treelike perches so this jungle cat can laze on the branches and

contemplate which antelope (or passing dog or human) he would like to pounce on next. (*Warning*: cats, even lionhearted ones, should not be allowed outdoors by themselves unless they are in an enclosure from which they can't escape and that predators can't enter.)

The love sponge: Have a lap? Then you have this cat in it. Have a computer keyboard? Then you have this cat on it. This cat's favorite enrichment activities will come from tactile experiences, such as being petted and cuddled, as well as having items of various textures added to his environment, such as sheepskins and plush toys.

The outgoing cat: This kitty loves to be the center of attention. At Thanksgiving, at least two items are guaranteed to be on the table— a turkey and your cat. The outgoing cat loves social activities in which he is the focus. Try trick training and games you can play together. Don't be surprised when you teach this cat to fetch better than the family dog does.

The perpetual kitten: Does your adult cat appear never to have left kittenhood behind? Does he constantly latch on to your ankle and refuse to let go, do daily battle with invisible butterflies, and demolish the holiday decorations year after year? This cat loves shiny things and moving toys. He will go gaga for a bird feeder set outside a window—just don't let him out to "play" with the visiting birds.

The professional sunbather: This kitty spends most of the day following sunbeams and napping in them. A professional sunbather will love window perches and beds strategically placed in his favorite spots.

This professional sunbather plies his trade on a comfy sunlit couch. Enrich your sun-loving cat with plenty of well-placed perches.

The shy cat: Any unusual sound or activity, however mild, will send this kitty scooting under the bed. No way, no how, is he going to greet household guests. Enrichment for the shy kitty is fairly easy—a maze of kitty condos and cardboard boxes for him to get lost in will soon become his favorite refuge.

The smarty pants: This cat is a clever escape artist. He can figure out how to open the pantry to get food, and you're pretty sure that if he had thumbs he'd take over the world. He's high in the bookshelf with your other cat, who's sleeping, while smarty pants is reading *Macbeth*. This kitty will love puzzle toys and motorized toys.

The territorial terror: This is a cat who knows what he wants—and what he wants is to have no other cats in his domain. If you add

The New Cat

Of course, when you first adopt a cat or a kitten you will not immediately know what he appreciates. Before you break the bank by buying all of the toys in sight, choose just a few standard *cat-cessories*, and see what your new kitty responds to. For starters, you might try some catnip, a food-dispensing toy, a feather toy, and a window perch. Observe how your cat interacts with them. By doing so, you will learn a great deal about his play preferences, and you will have a better idea about what he will find enriching.

Don't worry if it takes a while for your cat to open up and show his true personality; cats need time to adjust to new people and surroundings. Spend quality time with the latest addition to your household, and before too long, you will discover exactly what makes him twitch with excitement.

another cat (or small dog) to your territorial terror's home, the fur may fly. Give this cat lots of toys and novel scents to keep him occupied.

The three faces of kitty: He's unpredictable. One day he's a cuddle bug, the next he's ignoring you, and the day after that he is booking the next flight out of town. How do you entertain such a mercurial kitty? With a little bit of everything, of course! He's easy to entertain, even though he's not easy to read.

The tummy: "Food, more food, and where is the food?" That is this kitty's battle cry. To keep him from getting fat, use food as his plaything—placed inside toys, put on high perches., and scattered on the floor. Make him work for his keep!

By studying your cat, you can learn what will motivate him. When you find your cat's favorite enrichment activities, make them a regular part of his day. Be consistent—your cat will notice when you skip a regular activity. This is why it's good to have a variety of activities he can engage in and new toys on hand in case of an enrichment emergency, such as houseguests or an unexpected disruption of your regular routine.

Solo ENRICHMENT

Unless you have a "kitty cam," you're probably not completely sure what your cat is doing while you're away. Most likely, he's sleeping off a rough night of sleep. But some cats can get themselves into trouble, especially if enrichment activities are scarce. The evidence of a naughty (or bored or anxious) cat's activities only becomes clear when you come home to find a new pattern in your sofa (the ripped look isn't just for jeans, is it?), cat hair on your clean dishes (how did he open the dishwasher?), and some surprises next to the litter box, rather than in it.

Cats such as this one enjoy their lounging time. Yet they also need positive ways to entertain themselves while you're away.

To keep your feline companion out of trouble while he's on his own, you need to key into his natural instincts. Working for food—hunting, digging, ripping—is definitely on the top of the list. Cats are extremely skilled hunters, using keen senses to catch other animals, such as birds and rodents. Watching a house cat hunt is like getting a glimpse of a wild cat pursuing large game. Whatever the intended prey, cats are serious about stalking and hunting.

Cats have lots of fun pouncing on things as well, including balls, noisy toys, and prey toys. They also like batting around dangling toys. And don't forget that felines are pleasure lovers extraordinaire. They will revel in soft resting places, cushy perches, and scratching posts.

Will Work for Food

One natural daily activity that most house cats miss is the hunt for food. Handing a hunter a dish of food is almost insulting—and definitely boring. Feral cats will dig food out of garbage cans, dumps, and other such places, trying to get to the choicest pieces (or most edible anyway). So, enhance your cat's diet (and day) by giving him a chance to work for his food.

Hunting for Food

A cat in the wild can spend hours every day looking for food. A house cat spends just a few minutes on this most important aspect of his life. So, why not make eating a little more interesting for him? Here are some ways to turn food into a happy distraction.

Even if your cat's regular meal doesn't include dry food, you can supplement his diet (and his enrichment activities) by doing the kibble scatter with weight-controlled kibble or treats.

Hide-and-seek courses: For each meal, divide your cat's food allotment among a number of small containers, and set them out all over the house. Make sure to show your cat what you're doing the first few times. This makes eating more of a challenge for him because he must search for his food. Eating small portions is much healthier, and seeking out food can be helpful for weight loss. Once your cat understands that he has to search for his food, you can start placing the containers in different areas each day to make the hunt more challenging.

Kibble scatter: Instead of pouring your cat's kibble into a bowl, scatter it on the floor (where it's clean). Even if your cat's regular meal doesn't include dry food, you can supplement his diet (and his enrichment activities) by doing the kibble scatter with weight-control kibble or treats. Just don't offer too many extra calories, or your sleek feline may turn into a chubby kitty.

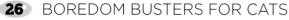

On a clean wooden floor, this hungry kitty gobbles up his scattered treats. The kibble scatter is a fun way to enliven mealtimes.

A puzzle toy captivates a curious kitty. Some puzzle toys use food, some use moving objects, and some use both to fascinate cats.

Sneaky snacks: As with your cat's regular meal, you can hide his snacks or treats all over the house and have him search for them. This is a particularly good trick to use just before you leave the house, especially if you have a nervous cat or one suffering from separation anxiety. It will distract your cat from your departure and give him something to do while you're away. Make sure to lead him to the snacks the first few times you do this so he understands the game. Use weight-control treats if necessary to prevent weight gain.

Digging, Ripping, and Puzzling for Food

Some cats aren't as into the hunt as others; some may even get bored by it. So instead of having him hunt for food, you can make him work for it in a different way. Let him dig his food out of toys or rip away a surprise package to get at the yummy goodness.

Food-dispensing toys: Dogs were the first to enjoy this type of toy, but several models made for cats have recently appeared on shelves of pet-supply stores. These toys come in a number of shapes, from balls and fish to cones, as well as in many materials, from pliable rubber to hard plastic. You can even divide your cat's daily food allotment among a few of these toys. Digging with tongue and paw to get his food will keep your cat happily occupied. Have several toys on hand so you can wash and dry a set while others are in use.

Food tear-aways: Does your cat like to wrestle or bunny kick? Then he'll love working on ripping open a wrapped present filled with his favorite food. Wrap his food or treats (you can include some catnip, too) in plain (no dyes) tissue paper, and tie it with a bit of twine. To bring out the hunter in your cat even more, tie the bundle to the end of a piece of string, then pull the goodies around to entice him. He'll be so intrigued that he'll *have* to have the package. Then you can watch him rip it up to his heart's content. (*Warning*: because of the string, you shouldn't leave him alone with this toy.)

Puzzle toys: There are a bunch of puzzle toys on the market that make your cat use his brainpower to get food out of them and some that will stimulate his prey drive. Your kitty may have to remove, spin, or slide pieces of the puzzle to locate the treats or get at the moving object. Such toys can keep your cat entertained for a long time!

🐾 Stalking

Stalking is a major part of hunting and is what generally takes the most time, skill, and brainpower. Don't skimp on the stalking aspect of your cat's hunting games. Make him work for whatever it is that he's hunting—whether it's a bundle of feathers on a string, a satchel of catnip, or a crinkly ball. Laser toys are also great for encouraging stalking behavior (see pages 44–45).

Kittens, like this one, may show early interest in stalking "prey." Let them stalk only in the house or in a safe outdoor enclosure.

Fascinated, this kitty bats at a swinging, feathered ball. This toy incorporates many of the features that will attract your cat.

Will Pounce for Fun

Once you've set about enriching the life of your kitten or cat, your house will probably look like you robbed a pet store. An active cat should have at least ten safe toys to play with at all times, with more toys waiting for rotation. Rotating toys is important (see "Avoiding the Boredom Stare," page 34). Here are some types of toys you should consider buying for your cat.

Ball toys: Balls make great prey—they roll, they are unpredictable, and many of the ones specifically for cats also make irresistible noises. They sometimes incorporate aspects to mimic birds or rodents, and some even move on their own (battery operated). Your feline's instinct to stalk and pounce will definitely be aroused.

Crinkle toys: Cats are suckers for sound; toys that make crinkly noises arouse your cat's hunting instinct. Some of them also include feathers, twine, catnip, and other cat-friendly materials. Need a toy on the cheap? Scrunch up a piece of scrap paper, and toss it to your cat. Ten minutes of fun for less than a penny!

Door-hanging toys: You haven't truly arrived as a besotted cat owner until you have a cat toy hanging from one or more of your doorknobs. Door-hanging toys are springy or have moving parts that simulate prey. Nothing says "I love my cat" more than decorating your doors for him!

Feather toys: It's a bird, it's a plane . . . no, it's feathers on a string. A bunch of feathers is irresistible for a cat. Just make sure they're not attached to a living bird. Want something cheap and easy? Get a peacock feather from a craft-supply store.

Noisy toys: Some toys play music, sing, or make animal sounds; others allow you to record your voice. These seem to capture the attention of some cats, even to the point of obsession. Oh, and don't forget bells!

Prey toys: No assortment of cat toys is complete without the requisite mouse toy.

Avoiding the Boredom Stare

Some cats get bored seeing the same toys every day and will eventually ignore them. To avoid that "I'm so bored" stare from your kitty, let him have only a few of his toys at any one time; put the rest away. Every couple of days, you can replace two or three of the toys that are out with others, putting the "old" ones away for a while.

Do not fall victim to the feline boredom stare. Protect yourself by rotating your cat's toys frequently so they stay "new."

These come in a seemingly endless array of forms, from the simple furry mouse to the more elaborate motorized rodent. Other moving toys, noisy toys, or those that feature preylike materials, such as feathers, are also considered prey toys.

Toilet paper: Toilet paper is fun (for your cat) to unravel but not so much fun (for you) to clean up. To prevent your cat from unraveling the toilet paper, get a cover for the roll—most people don't want feline enrichment to cause a toilet paper outage.

You can, however, save the empty tube for your cat's amusement.

For even more fun, tape one end with masking tape, put a couple of big marbles and catnip in the tube, and tape the other end. Voilà! An easy and cheap cat toy!

Will Revel for Pleasure

Anyone who's ever seen a cat stretched out on his back or snuggled into a soft corner knows these hunter-pouncers are pleasure lovers, too. So don't forget to provide for this particular aspect of their lives.

Cozy beds: Cats spend much of their lives napping and definitely appreciate dedicated napping space, especially if it's

The Bathtub Roll

Cats love toys that move and roll when they are pounced on, but these kinds of toys aren't much fun when they roll out of reach under the furniture. Put a few balls, giant marbles, and shiny, jingly toys into a dry bathtub, and show your cat that the toys are a great deal more fun when they can't get away. However, unless you like being woken up to the sound of marbles on porcelain, remember to remove the toys from the bathtub until after your morning shower. Or use only sponge balls—sans the bells.

This tabby cat enjoys the soft texture of a bed quilt as he snuggles in for a lazy afternoon. Cats revel in plush beds and toys.

plush and cozy. Bolster and donut beds are good for cats who like to curl into a ball, and what cat doesn't love a sheepskin rug?

Plush toys: Plush toys for cats often have a space you can fill with catnip. Plush toys aren't typically thought of as ideal for cats, but some adore—and adopt—them.

Wool toys: Cats love felted wool, probably because of the natural animal scent and texture. An easy, inexpensive way to make a toy close to felted wool is to wash a wool sweater a few times in very hot water and put it in the dryer. Cut the sweater into small pieces, and offer them to your cat. If you can sew (even a little), put a pinch of catnip and/or a bell into the center of a piece of the felted sweater and sew it up—instant irresistible cat toy!

Kitty Supervision

Keeping your furry friend safe is the most important part of any enrichment activity. When it comes to toy safety, know your cat. If he likes to bat and chase, then most commercial cat toys are probably safe for solo play. If your cat's habit is to destroy or ingest materials, closely watch all toy play. All cats should be supervised when toys have strings or detachable parts. In addition, check that the plants your cat is exposed to are nontoxic, and if you take him outdoors, keep him in a safe enclosure or on a leash.

Social ENRICHMENT

There's little that is more fulfilling for a cat than one-on-one time with his favorite human—well, depending on the cat. Some felines would prefer stalking birds in the yard, which could also be considered social (though not so much for the birds). However, cats are safer indoors. Spending time in your presence makes your cat feel secure and keeps him occupied and out of trouble. If he also likes to play with other people and with animal pals, that can be enriching for him too. Here are some social activities that could enrich your cat's life.

For the Two of You

Despite their love of indolent lounging, cats do not like slipping into bubble baths. A shower of catnip-scented bubbles, however, is another kettle of soap! Chasing those heavenly smelling soapy spheres, playing fetch (yes, really), and pouncing on elusive laser points are among the many games you can enjoy with your cat

Bubble chase: You can blow catnip-scented bubbles for your kitty, who, like kids and dogs, may be fascinated by bubbles. Pet-specific bubbles are tougher than regular soap ones so they don't pop as easily, even when they hit the ground, which gives most cats time to pounce.

Fetch: Believe it or not, cats can be taught to fetch a light object that's easy to pick up, such as a crinkle ball. In fact, in most cases, your cat will teach you the game by bringing you something to toss for him. The game usually goes on for a while, then a cat will get bored and move on to something else—generally a nap. To teach your cat how to fetch, toss the ball to him, and encourage him to bring it back to you by calling his name and holding out a treat. Trade the treat for the ball. Continue this until your cat starts to understand the game. Then add the word *fetch* after you toss the ball. Eventually he will come to associate *fetch* with the activity of bringing back the ball—or not!

Hide-and-seek: Hide somewhere in your home, and call your cat—don't go too far the first time. When he finds you, reward him with something he likes, such as a treat

This cat seems to be patiently awaiting the perfect bubble to pounce on. Cat-specific bubbles are great for social enrichment.

or petting. This can be a fun game for cats, who are natural stalkers. Gradually increase the distance you hide from your cat to make the game more difficult.

Laser toys: Are you and your cat still playing with bits of string? Leap into the twenty-first century by tossing that string into the recycle bin and replacing it with a laser toy. You can use any laser pointer (think PowerPoint presentation) to beam the little red dot on the ground and walls and have your cat chase it. There's even a toy that moves the laser around the floor and walls on its own; you can turn on its timer and set the device on a counter to run (although that may be more solo than social enrichment). After each ten-minute game, give your cat a treat or a favorite toy so he doesn't get frustrated. After all, the laser point isn't tangible, and at the end of each hunting session, your cat really just wants to be able to catch something.

Walking on a leash: Most cats will not suffer the indignity of walking on a leash. A cat is not a dog. Actually, not walking well on a leash has less to do with a cat's pride than it does with his nature. Cats are territorial, so taking a cat outside of his territory can be frightening for him. Even taking a cat on a leash to the far end of a yard can be scary because there are outdoor-cat scents there, marked by cats that your cat does not know. Now your cat is in another feline's territory. Is it safe to be there? Will there be a fight?

This is why most cats are not going to be in love with the idea of walking on a leash.

The Trainable Cat

Training cats is becoming more common. Be warned, however, that some cats will not take to formal training at all. If you're lucky enough to have one who does, then by all means start training! You and your cat will spend valuable time together, enhancing both of your lives. Keep training sessions short—ten to fifteen minutes—and make them fun and positive. Some cats react well to clicker training, which uses a type of noisemaker and treats to elicit certain behaviors. You can teach a cat appropriate behavior or to give you a paw, roll over, sit up, and even jump through hoops—really!

On the other paw, there are cats who adore having some safe time outside, especially as you will be there to supervise. Starting leash training when your cat is young is the key to success in leash walking.

Here are a few important safety tips for walking your indoor cat outside on a leash:

- Always use a harness when walking a cat. Make sure that the harness fits snugly and that the cat can't back out of it if he becomes scared and panics.
- Have a collar with ID tags on your cat at all times.
- Have your cat microchipped in case he does escape from you and his collar falls off.
- Use flea and tick protection.

Wand toys: Stick just about anything on the end of a fishing pole–type contraption, and you've got a great cat toy. You can choose from among a variety of wand toys at your local pet shop, or you can get creative and make your own. Find a branch, a yardstick, or something similar, then tie a piece of fishing line or twine to one end. At the end of the line, tie on a piece of cardboard, a bit of pipe cleaner, and a feather. Violà! You have a cheap and easy cat toy that you can use to enhance your cat's hunting instinct—and help him burn a few extra calories.

Animal Pals at Home

A fun way to enrich your cat socially is to provide him with a friend or his very own companion animal. Because cats are, by nature, territorial, many will not want an interloper of the same species but may take to a member of another species. However, kittens raised together or cats carefully introduced to each other often appreciate having a feline "sibling" in the house.

Canine companion: A number of cats do appreciate dogs. It doesn't have to be war—at times, a cat's best friend is canine. Before you get your cat a canine companion, determine whether the dog would be appreciated, simply tolerated, or outright rejected. Has your cat ever interacted with a dog? Do you think that he'll be afraid? Will the dog terrorize the cat, or the other way around? It's a judgment call only you can make by evaluating the personalities of your cat and the new dog. Most cats and dogs, when introduced at a young age, get along quite well.

Feline friend: Many cats get along well with other cats and may like having one (or more) as a housemate. Most of us have seen the disturbing news footage of people who have 200 cats in one house—not a good practice, so don't try this at home (even if you could afford the food and vet fees)! However, it's not unusual for the average cat-owning household to have 2 to 4 cats without any problems.

If you do want a household with multiple cats, it's best to introduce them to each other when they are young. If you have an older cat who has never lived around another cat, he might have territorial issues. If your house is large enough, even territorial cats can get

This feline and his canine buddy show that cats and dogs can be pals. Before you get a dog, find out if your kitty is canine friendly.

Catnip

Oh, the joys of catnip! No one really knows exactly how it works to make cats go wacky, drool profusely, and appear to be high. The theory is that there's a chemical in the herb that triggers something in the cat's brain, causing a temporary reaction. After a few minutes, the cat resumes normal activity. It takes thirty minutes to a couple of hours for the catnip effect to "reboot," and then it will work on the cat again. Most cats are sensitive to catnip, although some are not, and it doesn't work on kittens younger than six months. Humans don't react to catnip in the same way (obviously), but in some cultures, it is used in tea as a very mild sedative. Catnip is a great enrichment tool to use during your social time together. It is not addictive nor does it have any kind of lasting effect on your cat. He might ask to borrow your Grateful Dead albums, but that's about it.

along by establishing a kind of pecking order. Then again, dealing with a pecking order isn't enriching—it's annoying. However, most cats will get along if there's enough food and attention to go around. If you want to adopt another cat to enrich your resident cat's life, follow the instructions in the box at right.

Fishy fascinators: It's ill advised to get rodents or birds to enrich (or entertain) cats, although small pets would be endlessly entertaining—for the cat. Having birds and rodents living in a household with cats is often a recipe for disaster. Instead, consider a fish tank, also entertaining for your cat and way less dangerous for the fish (and cat) as long as the tank is securely covered. This can provide many hours of watching and stalking fun. Don't want to take care of fish? A fish tank with lots of bubbles and some swaying plastic plants will do the trick as well.

Introducing Cats

Put the new cat in his own room, with a closed door between him and your resident cat. Give each a pet blanket with the other's scent so they get accustomed to the new smell. At first, let the cats only sniff at each other under the door. After a couple days, open the door, and let the cats interact for a short time. Give extra treats to make it a positive experience. Soon the cats should be coexisting peacefully and may become good play pals.

Environmental ENRICHMENT

ondos, DVDs and videotapes, mazes, perches, plants, scents—the possibilities for purr-inducing additions to enrich your cat's environment are intriguing, numerous, and varied. Environmental enrichment is all about providing your pet with areas that are meant just for him, appealing to and stimulating his natural instincts. Doing so can be as simple as offering your cat a lined wicker basket to curl up in or as elaborate as planting a kitty garden for his sniffing pleasure.

Baskets: Cats and baskets go together like peanut butter and jelly—but fortunately the cat-basket combo is a lot less sticky. Put some inexpensive baskets around your home to serve as sleeping and play areas for your kitty. Wicker baskets and plastic laundry baskets are particularly appreciated—especially when the clean laundry is still inside. (Bonus points if you can teach your cat to fold your underwear.) If you want to save yourself a lot of rewashing, fill these baskets with old clothes you don't mind having covered in cat fur!

Boxes and bags: You know how kids often prefer to play with the big cardboard box rather than with whatever came inside it? So does your cat. Place some boxes and big empty paper bags (not lunch-size ones) around your house for hours of kitty fun or places for a catnap or two.

Make sure the bags don't have handles, however, or your cat may get caught in them and panic. Some people might think that would make for a funny Web video, but your cat can be seriously hurt, so absolutely no handles on the bags. Even more important, do not let your cat play with plastic bags!

Condos: Cats feel safe when they have places in which to hide. Kitty condos, those treelike structures commonly covered in carpeting or sisal, double as hiding places and scratching posts. You can find these kitty condos in most pet stores as well as on the

A shy feline investigates a new hiding place. Small tents and flexible tubes make attractive escapes for your furry friend.

At any toy store you can find flexible tubes and small tents made for kids that are also great for cats to play in. Get a few of them, and put them together in a room to create a feline-fascinating maze.

Internet. The more cats you have, the larger and more elaborate your kitty condo probably should be.

DVDs and videotapes: There are DVDs and videotapes that have been put together just for cats; these programs feature birds, bubbles, fellow felines, fish, rodents, and all sorts of other stuff that cats love to watch. Whenever you are getting ready to leave the house, pop one of these in to entertain your stay-at-home kitty. Consider it the fishing channel for cats.

Mazes: At any toy store you can find flexible tubes and small tents made for kids that are also great for cats to play in. Get a few of them, and put them together in a room to construct a feline-fascinating maze. Add some cardboard boxes, and you've created a bit of heaven at home for your cat, especially if he's shy and likes places to hide.

Outdoor enclosures: Indoor-only cats stare endlessly outside at all of the action that they seem to be missing. You can give your kitty a little taste of the

✿ Scents

Catnip isn't the only scent our feline companions like. Visit a local pet store that sells holistic products, and buy a few scents to experiment with—usually you can purchase herbal or floral extracts in spray form. Try barley, chamomile, and valerian, to begin with. Spray the scents inside a brown paper bag, and watch your cat's reaction. If he likes it, he will carry the bag around the house and most likely drool on it. You should avoid all citrus scents—cats just don't like them.

outdoors—safely—with a cat enclosure. It can be as simple as a large cage that you attach to a kitty door or to a window-access point, or it can be as elaborate as a series of wire tunnels winding though your yard and up the side of your house.

Perches: Window perches are a must for any cat household, especially if your windowsills aren't wide enough to comfortably and safely hold a sleeping feline. A cat window perch basically extends the sill and creates a comfy, usually plush, area for kitty to laze the days away. If you want to get fancy, buy a heated window perch so your cat can warm his buns on chilly afternoons.

Plants: Cats love plants—often too much so for the health of your houseplants. Save them by creating a garden that's "kitty

Looking quite content, a kitty lies on a perch near a window. Give your cat a view of the great outdoors from a favored perch.

friendly." There are some easy-to-cultivate plants most cats will love—let your cat eat these plants, dig them up, whatever he likes. Use soil free of pesticides, fungicides, and other chemicals. Some plants your kitty might enjoy include barley, caraway, catnip, dill, echinacea, millet, mint, oats, valerian, and wheat grass. (*Warning*: Be aware that certain plants are toxic for cats; your kitty should be kept away from these at all times. See the American Society for the Prevention of Cruelty to Animals Web site—www .aspca.org—for a list of poisonous plants.)

Scratching areas: If your kitty lives to scratch—or even if he's just a part-time scratcher—you will want to provide him with all kinds of scratching areas in all types of textures. Try cardboard and sisal.

The Sport of Agility

The sport of agility started with dogs—modeled after equestrian events in which horses jump over a series of fences. The canine community modified it to include weave poles, A-frames, tunnels, and other obstacles. The dog must finish the course as quickly and as completely as possible. Should dogs have all the fun? No way! The feline community has further modified the sport of agility for cats. All it takes is an athletic, motivated cat and a patient, equally motivated trainer. This is a very fun and enriching activity for both cats and humans.

Enriched Cat, HAPPY CAT

Varying your cat's life just a little bit will help keep him from becoming bored. Don't vary his life or environment too much, however; cats do like routine. You might love a vacation to Tahiti to keep things fresh, but your cat will probably be happy with a new treat, toy, or window perch. Try to find at least three enrichment activities from each category, and apply them regularly to your cat's daily life. Not only will these activities keep him entertained, fit, and out of trouble, but they also may add years to his life. A happy cat is a healthy cat—and a healthy cat has a happy owner.

About the Author

Nikki Moustaki, freelance writer and animal trainer, has published more than forty books, primarily on the care and training of pets. She hosts two pet-related shows in Miami Beach, Florida, and hosted the NBC/MSN online show *The Celebrity Pet Dish*. Her Web site, The Pet Postcard Project (www.petpostcardproject.com), raises awareness, food, and funds for shelter animals. Nikki splits her time between New York City and Miami Beach with her two rescued Schnauzers, Pepper and Ozzie; a pound-puppy Schnoodle, Pearl; and three parrots. You can reach Nikki at www.nikkimoustaki.com.

Resources

Books and Magazines

BowTie Press (books on cats and cat care):

www.bowtiepress.com

CAT FANCY magazine: www.catchannel.com

Cat Organizations

The Cat Fanciers' Organization: www.cfainc.org

The National Cat Protection Organization:

www.saveacat.org

Sports Organizations

Feline Agility Competition: http://agility.cfa.org

International Cat Agility Tournaments:

www.catagility.com